1 PIANO, 4 HANDS

PIANO DUET PLAY·ALONG
VOLUME 2

MOVIE FAVORITES

2   CHARIOTS OF FIRE

8   THE ENTERTAINER
    from *The Sting*

20 THEME FROM "JURASSIC PARK"

26 MY FATHER'S FAVORITE
    from *Sense and Sensibility*

32 MY HEART WILL GO ON
    (LOVE THEME FROM 'TITANIC')

46 SOMEWHERE IN TIME

52 STAR TREK® THE MOTION PICTURE

60 YOU MUST LOVE ME
    from *Evita*

PLAYBACK+
Speed · Pitch · Balance · Loop

To access audio, visit:
www.halleonard.com/mylibrary

Enter Code
6952-5704-3313-7838

ISBN 978-1-4234-2126-9

Visit Hal Leonard Online at
www.halleonard.com

Contact us:
Hal Leonard
7777 West Bluemound Road
Milwaukee, WI 53213
Email: info@halleonard.com

In Europe, contact:
Hal Leonard Europe Limited
42 Wigmore Street
Marylebone, London, W1U 2RN
Email: info@halleonardeurope.com

In Australia, contact:
Hal Leonard Australia Pty. Ltd.
4 Lentara Court
Cheltenham, Victoria, 3192 Australia
Email: info@halleonard.com.au

CHARIOTS OF FIRE
from CHARIOTS OF FIRE

SECONDO

Music by VANC

Moderately (♩=72)

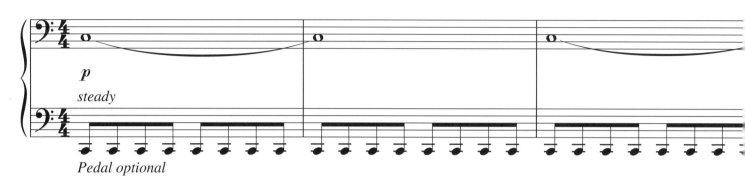

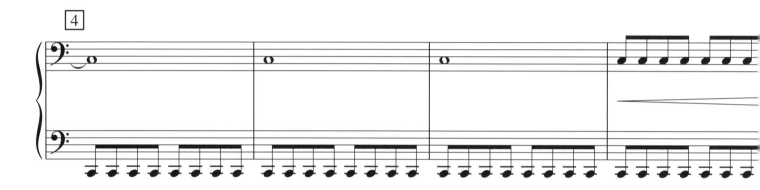

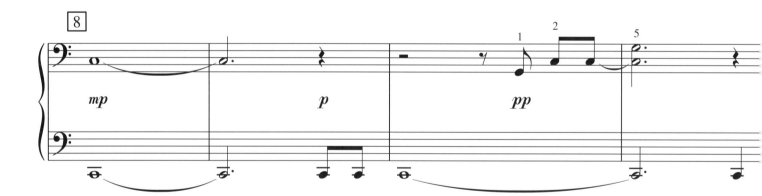

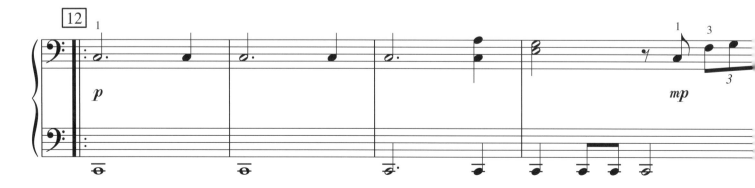

CHARIOTS OF FIRE
from CHARIOTS OF FIRE

PRIMO

Music by VANGELIS

Moderately (♩=72)

SECONDO

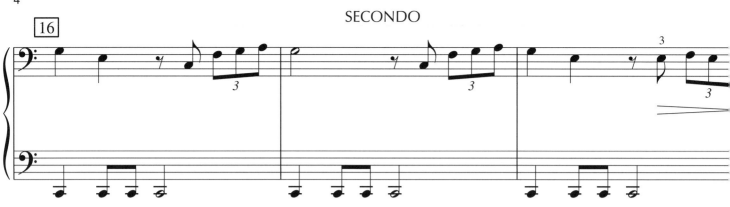

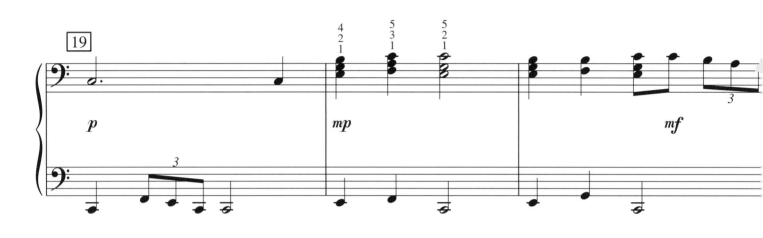

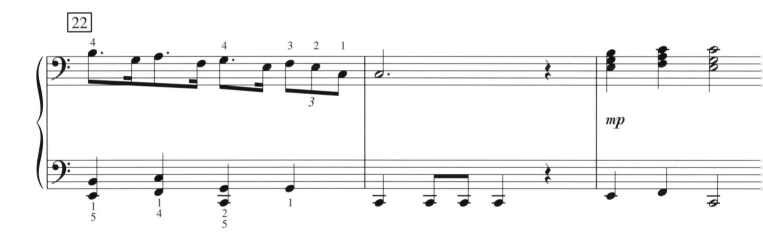

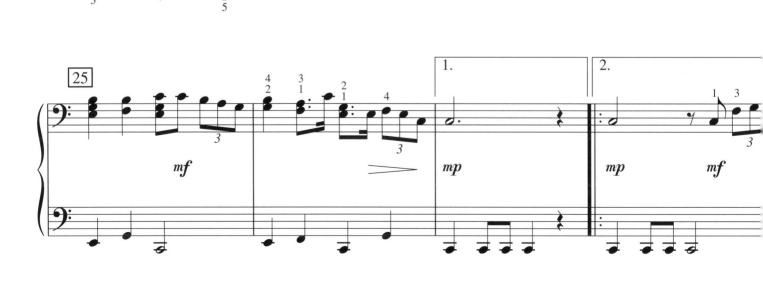

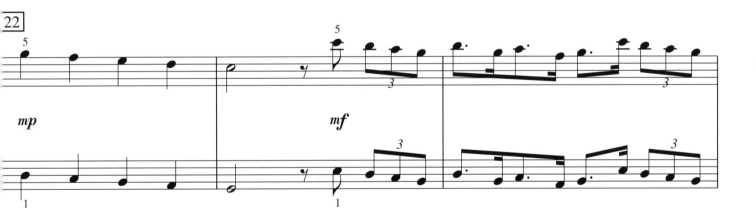

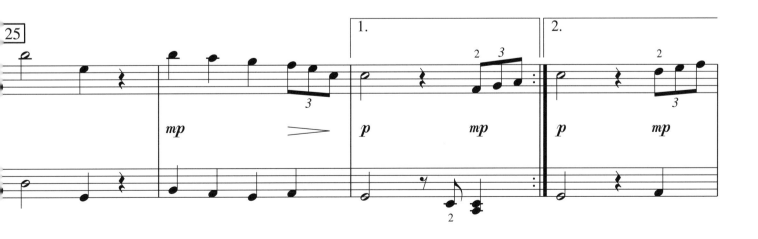

SECONDO

Add pedal to end

PRIMO

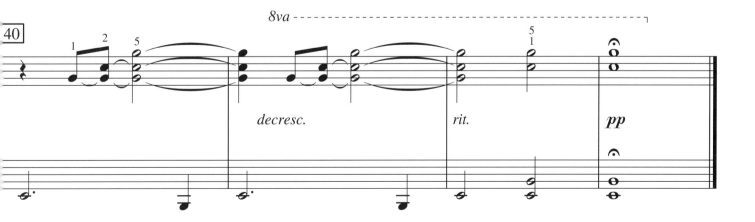

THE ENTERTAINER

featured in the Motion Picture THE STING

SECONDO

By SCOTT J[...]

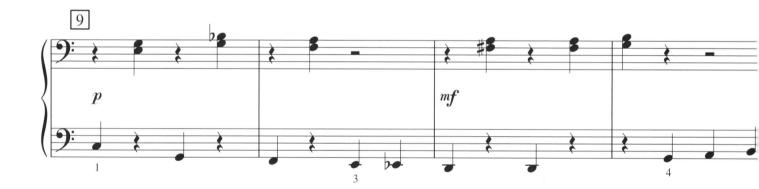

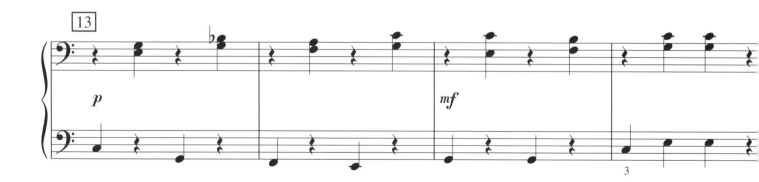

THE ENTERTAINER
featured in the Motion Picture THE STING

PRIMO

By SCOTT JOPLIN

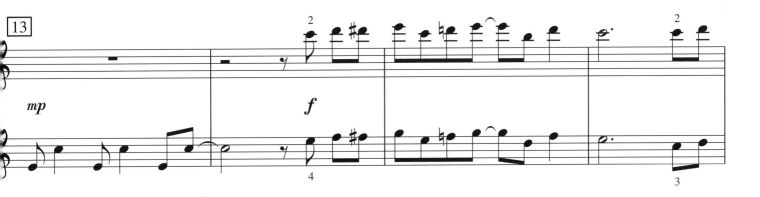

SECONDO

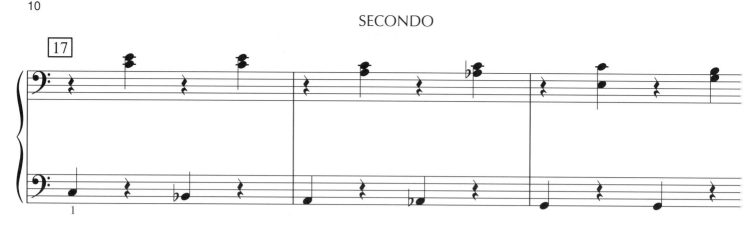

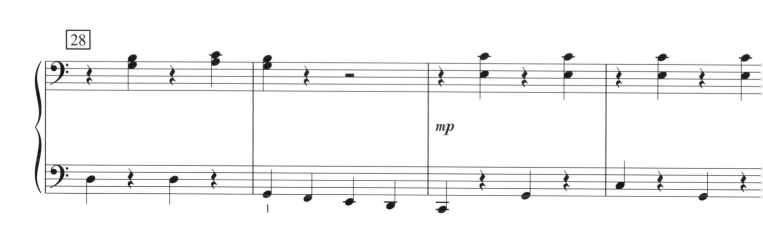

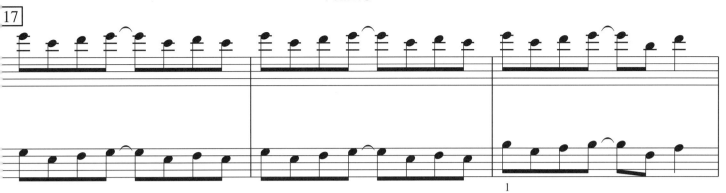

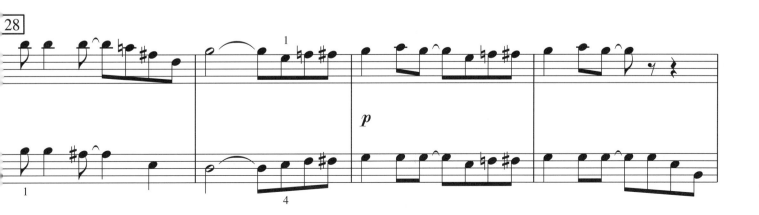

SECONDO

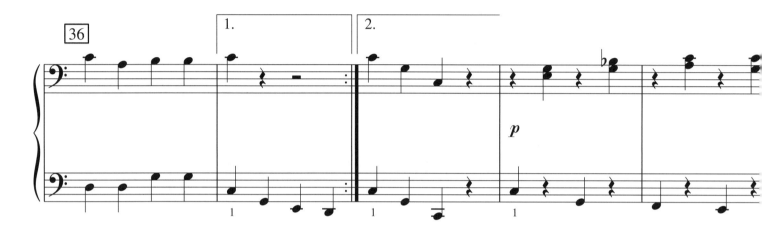

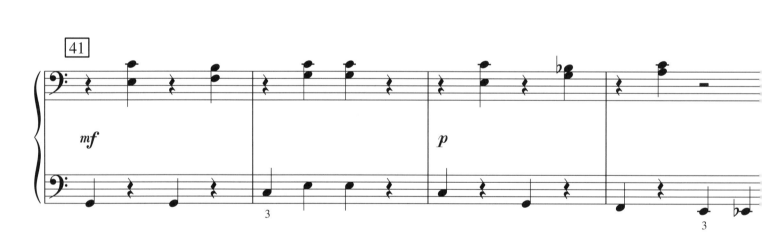

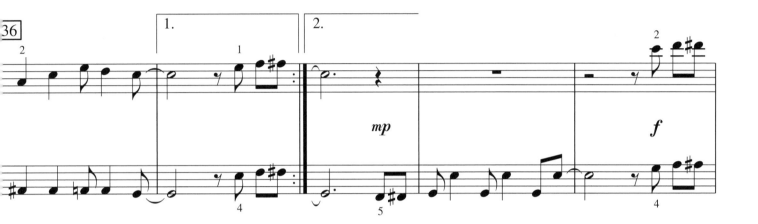

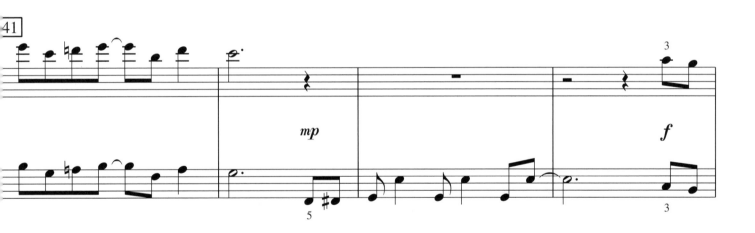

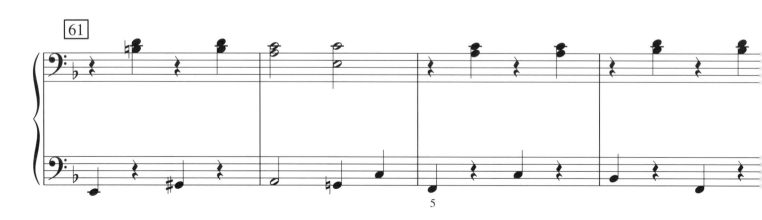

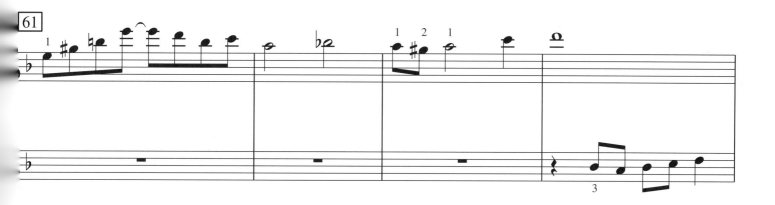

SECONDO

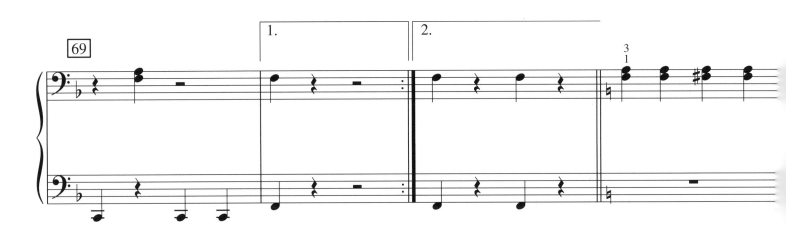

SECONDO

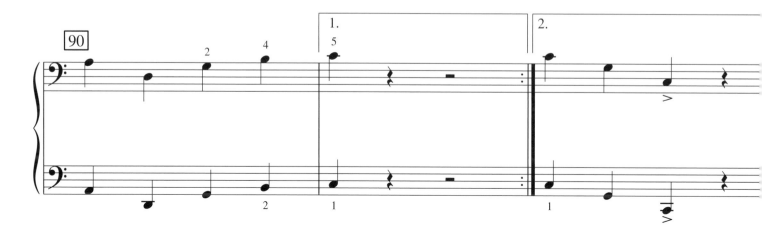

THEME FROM "JURASSIC PARK"

from the Universal Motion Picture JURASSIC PARK

SECONDO

Composed by JOHN WILLIAMS

Reflectively

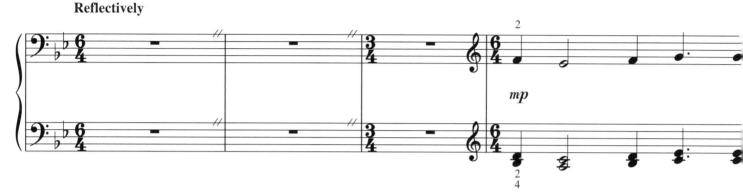

THEME FROM "JURASSIC PARK"

from the Universal Motion Picture JURASSIC PARK

PRIMO

Composed by JOHN WILLIAMS

Reflectively

SECONDO

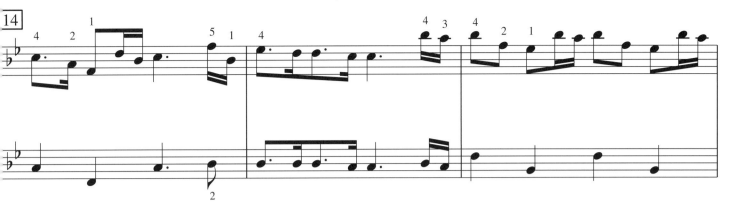

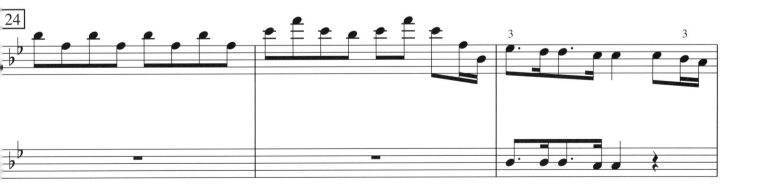

SECONDO

27

30

33

37

MY FATHER'S FAVORITE
from SENSE AND SENSIBILITY

SECONDO

By PATRICK DO...

Moderately slow

p expressively

With pedal

MY FATHER'S FAVORITE

from SENSE AND SENSIBILITY

PRIMO

By PATRICK DOYLE

Moderately slow

mp expressively

p

SECONDO

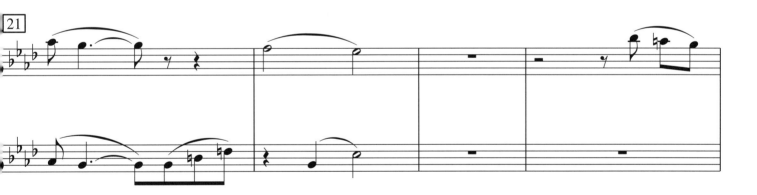

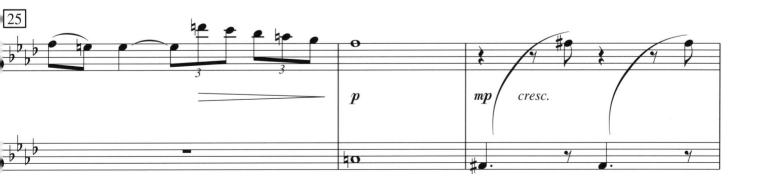

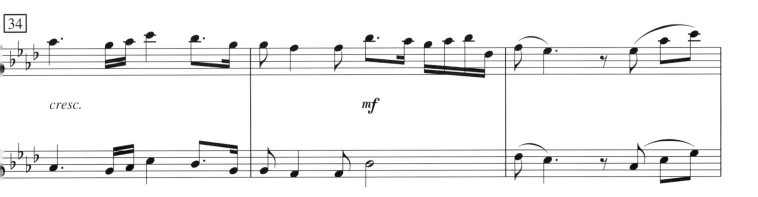

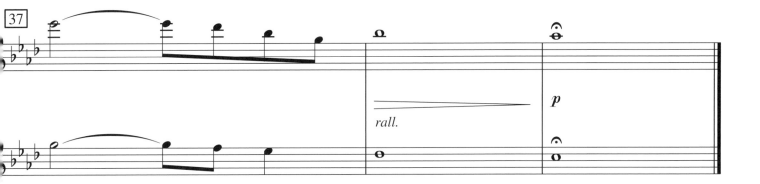

MY HEART WILL GO ON
(Love Theme from 'Titanic')
from the Paramount and Twentieth Century Fox Motion Picture TITANIC

SECONDO

Music by JAMES HORNER
Lyric by WILL JENNINGS

Moderately

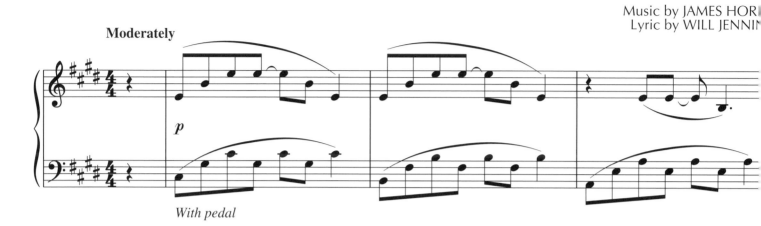

p

With pedal

cresc.

mf *dim.*

p

MY HEART WILL GO ON
(Love Theme from 'Titanic')
from the Paramount and Twentieth Century Fox Motion Picture TITANIC

PRIMO

Music by JAMES HORNER
Lyric by WILL JENNINGS

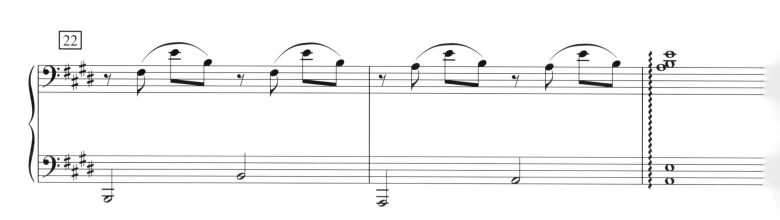

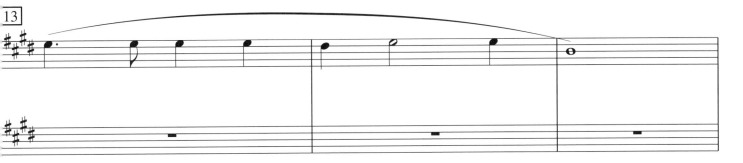

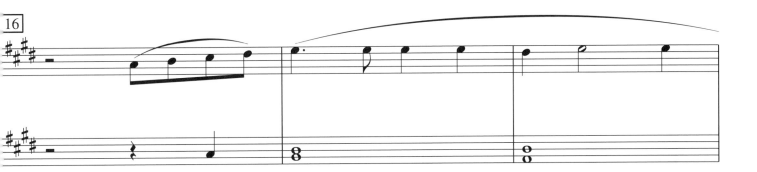

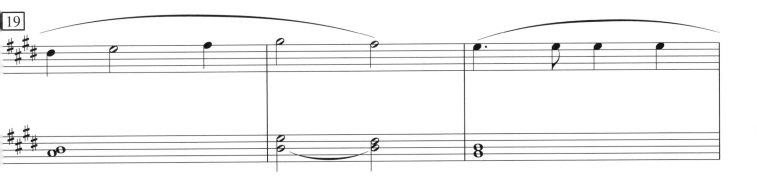

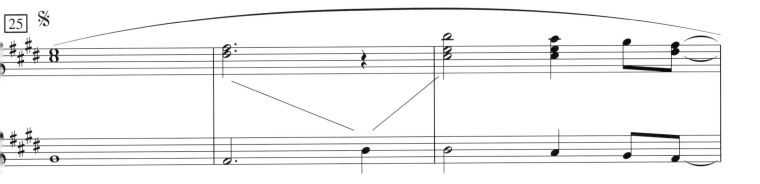

SECONDO

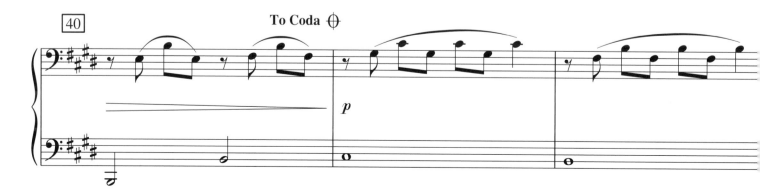

PRIMO

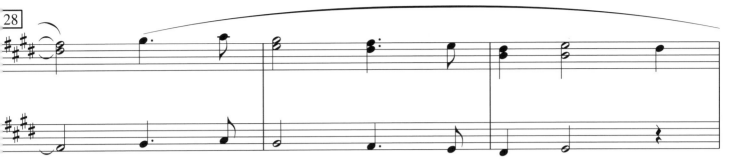

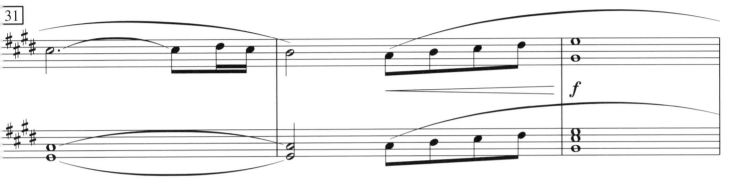

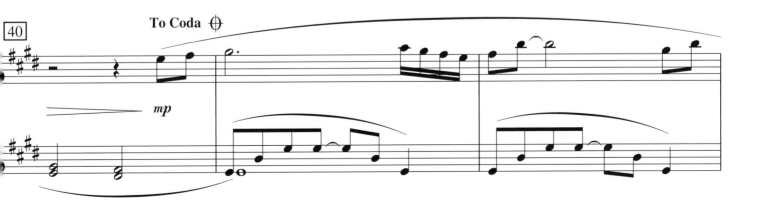

SECONDO

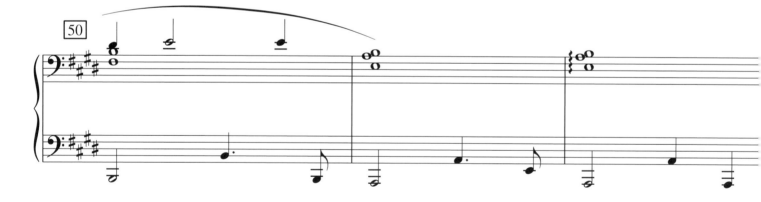

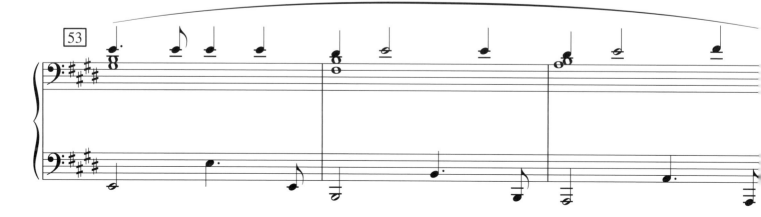

PRIMO

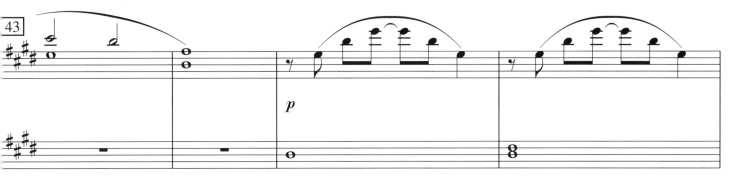

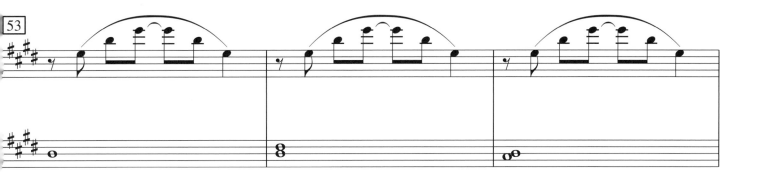

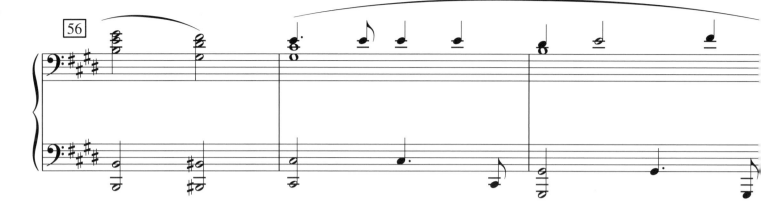

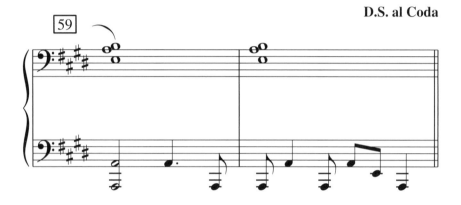

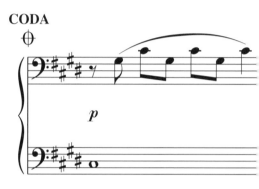

D.S. al Coda

CODA

p

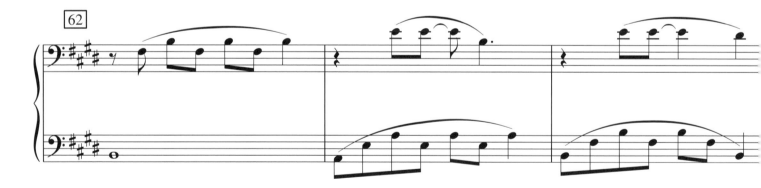

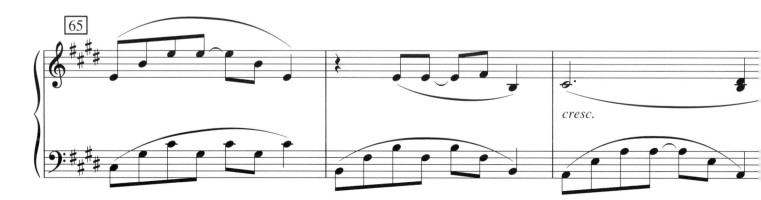

cresc.

PRIMO

D.S. al Coda   **CODA**

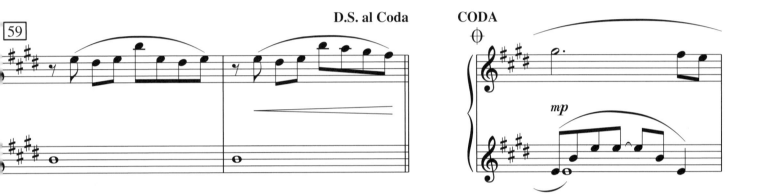

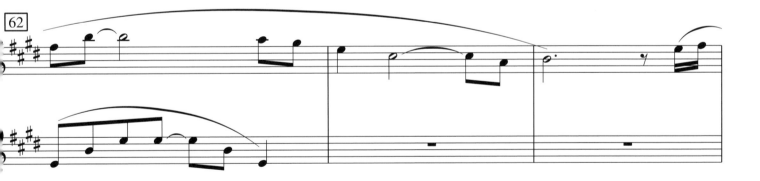

cresc.

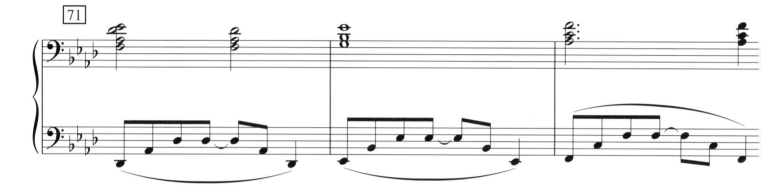

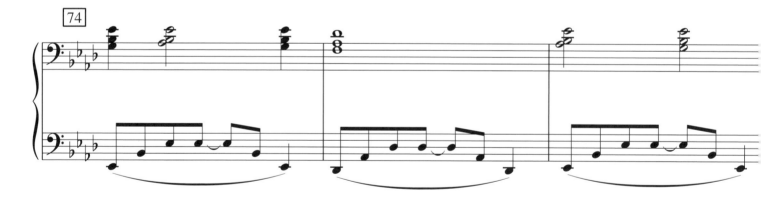

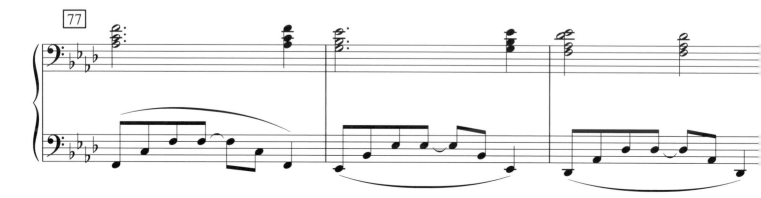

PRIMO

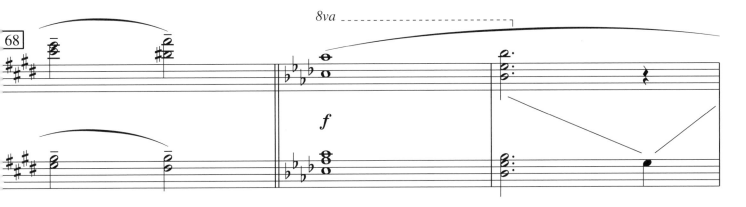

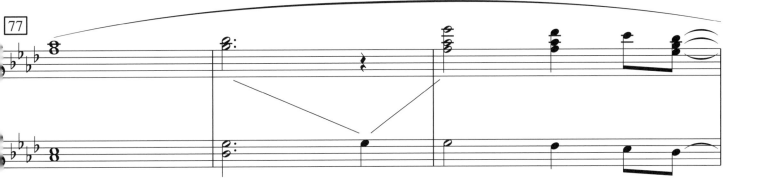

SECONDO

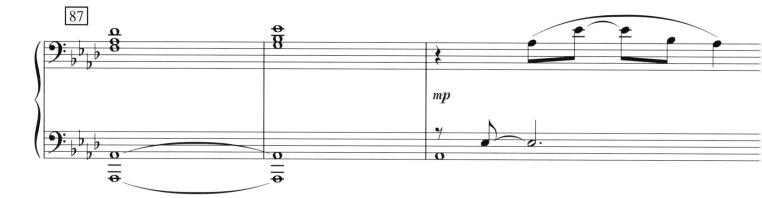

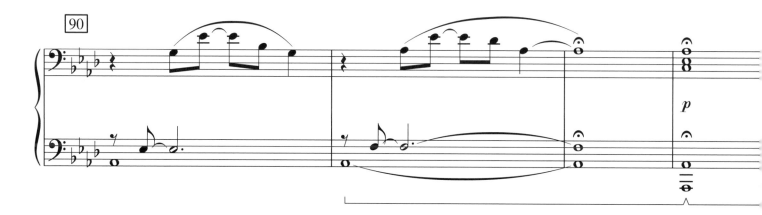

PRIMO

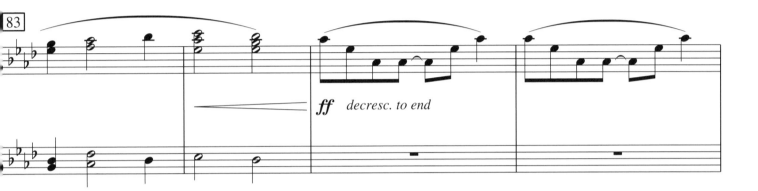

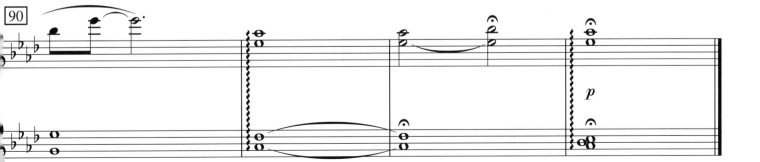

SOMEWHERE IN TIME

from SOMEWHERE IN TIME

SECONDO

By JOHN BA[...]

Moderately slow

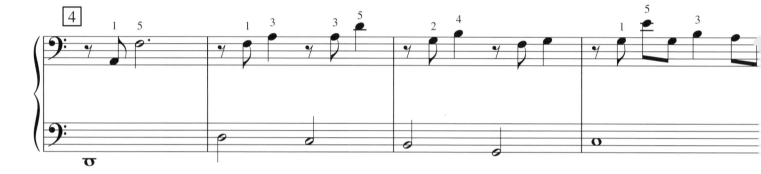

SOMEWHERE IN TIME
from SOMEWHERE IN TIME

PRIMO

By JOHN BARRY

Moderately slow

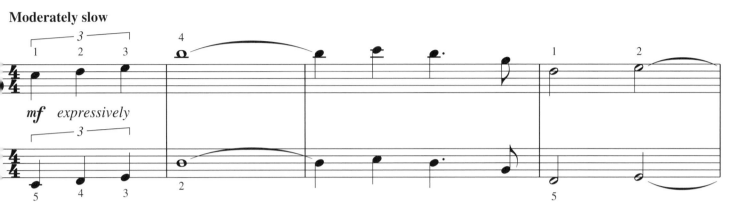

mf expressively

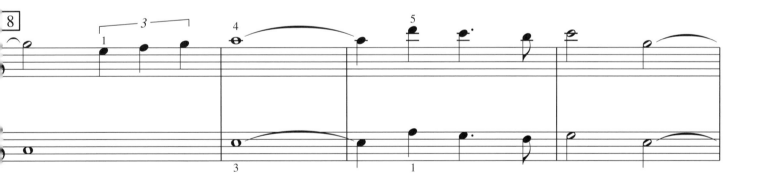

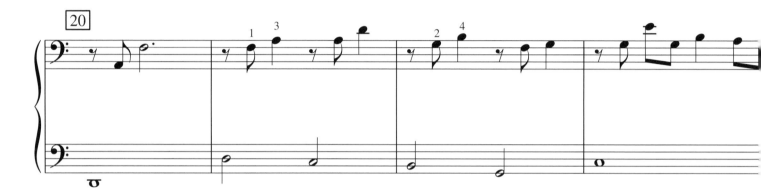

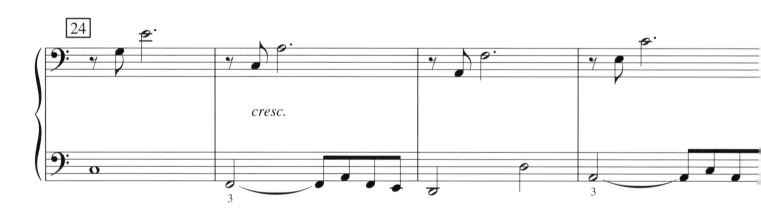

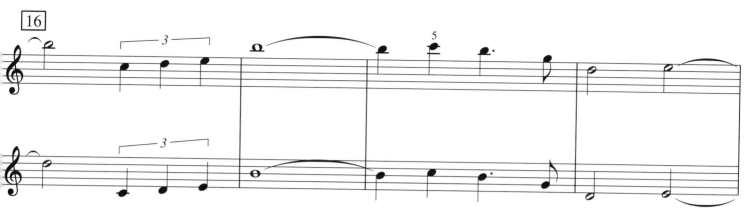

SECONDO

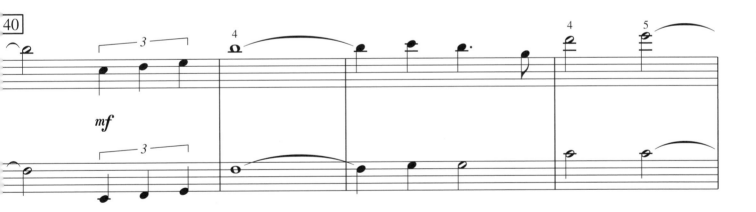

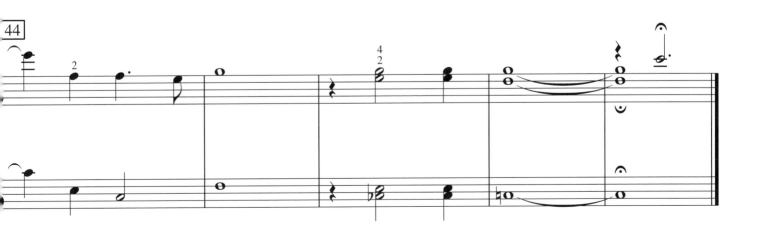

STAR TREK® THE MOTION PICTURE

Theme from the Paramount Picture STAR TREK: THE MOTION PICTURE

SECONDO

Music by JERRY GOLDSM

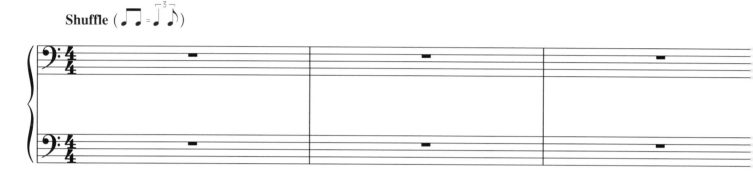

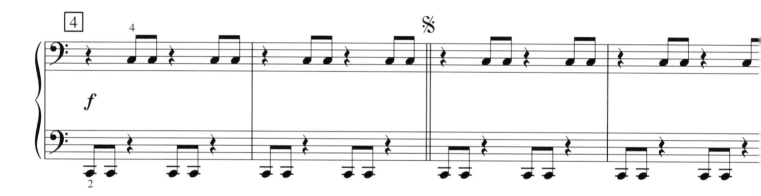

STAR TREK® THE MOTION PICTURE

Theme from the Paramount Picture STAR TREK: THE MOTION PICTURE

SECONDO

Music by JERRY GOLDSMITH

Shuffle

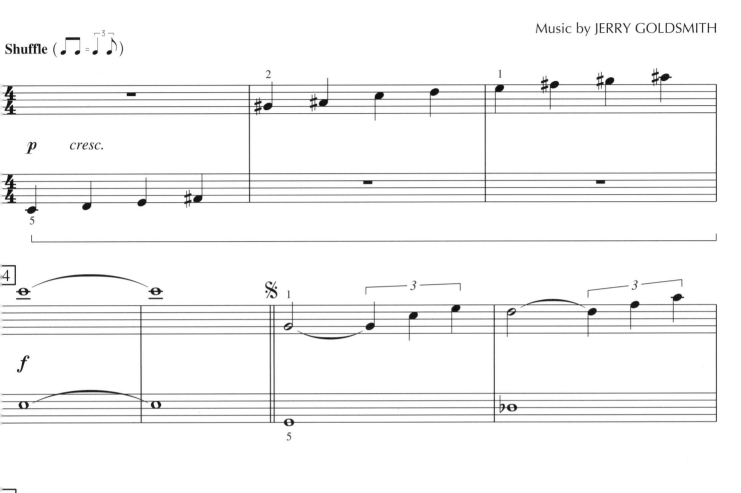

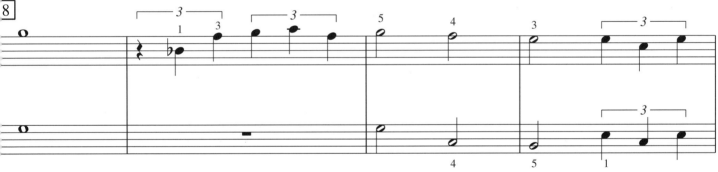

SECONDO

PRIMO

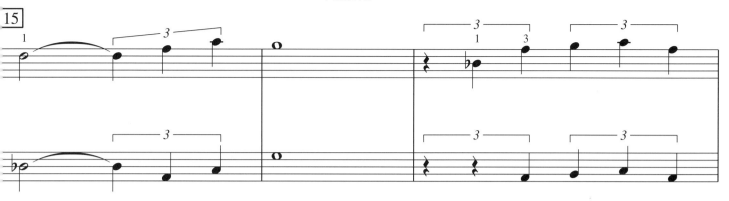

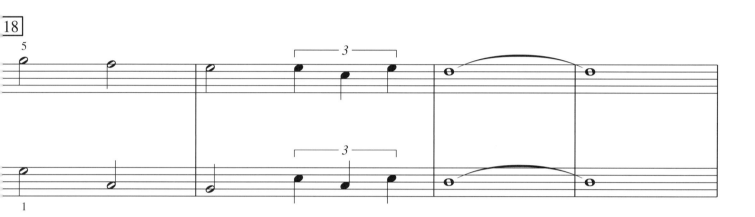

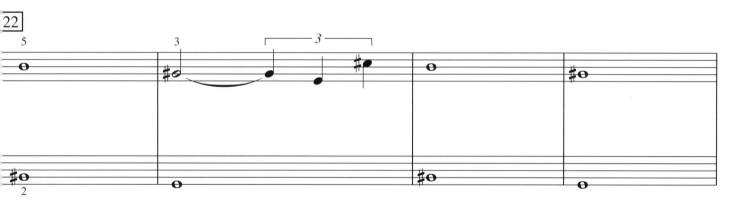

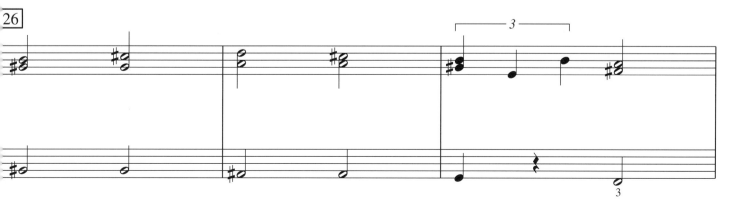

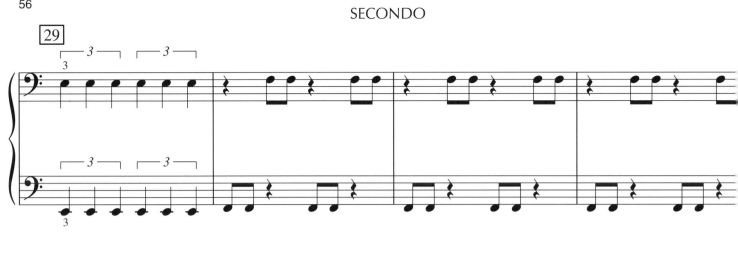

PRIMO

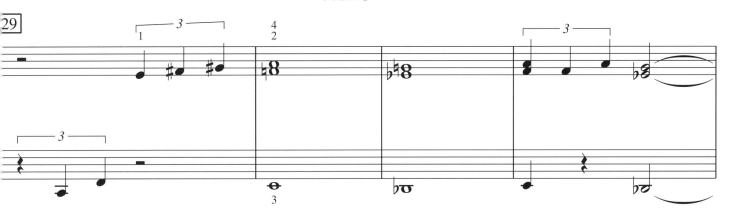

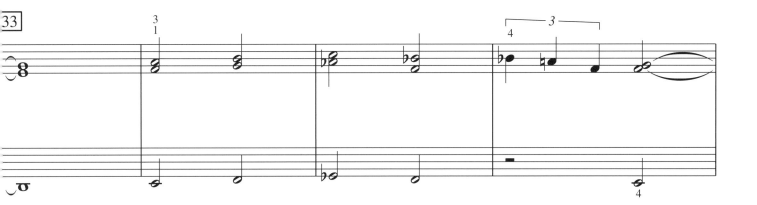

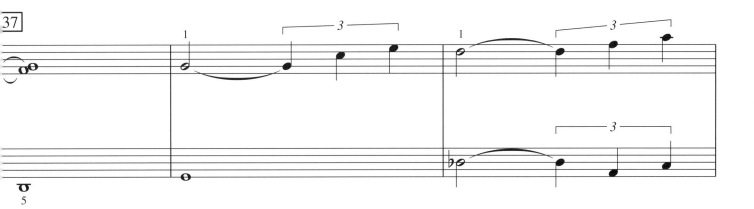

SECONDO

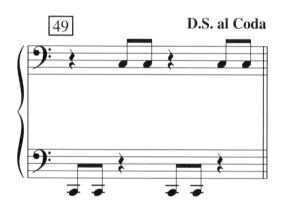
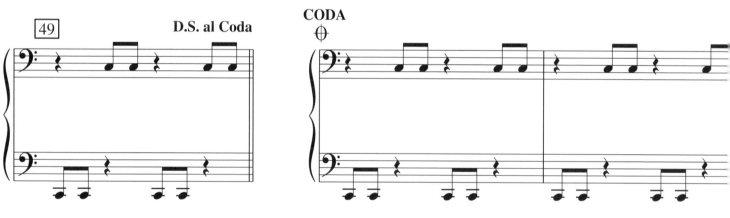

CODA

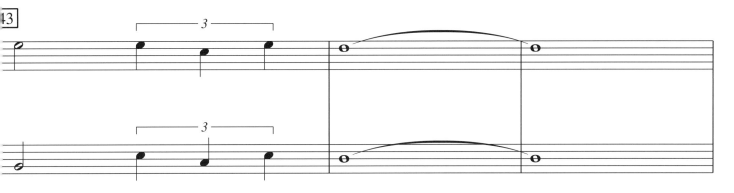

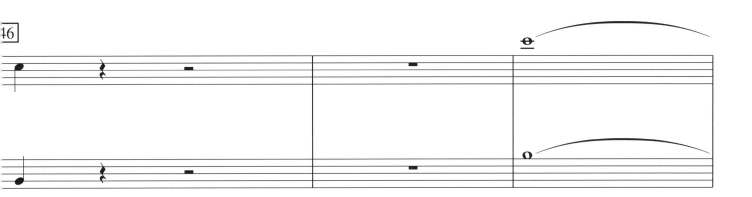

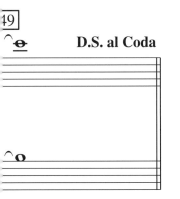

D.S. al Coda

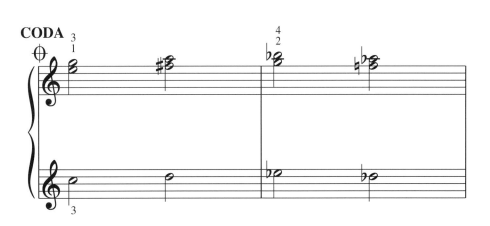

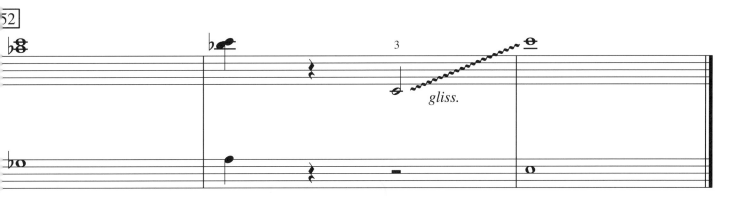

YOU MUST LOVE ME

from the Cinergi Motion Picture EVITA

SECONDO

Words by TIM
Music by ANDREW LLOYD WE

Flowing

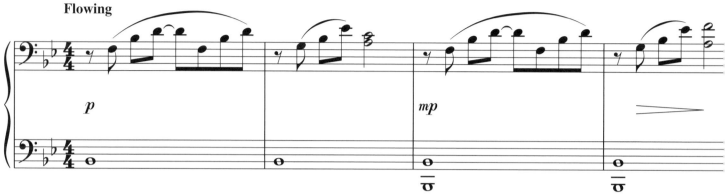

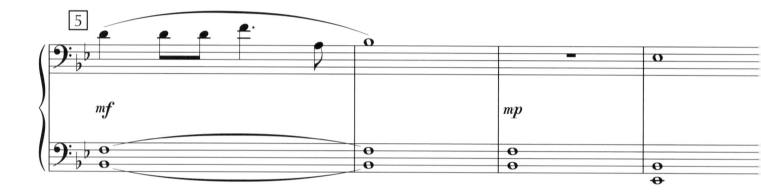

YOU MUST LOVE ME

from the Cinergi Motion Picture EVITA

PRIMO

Words by TIM RICE
Music by ANDREW LLOYD WEBBER

Flowing

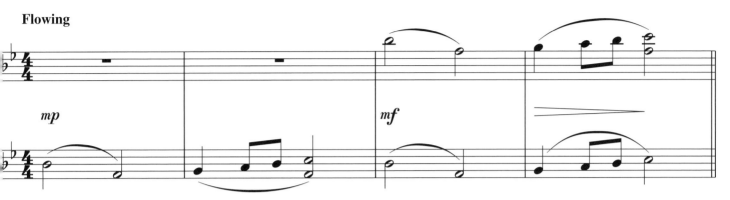

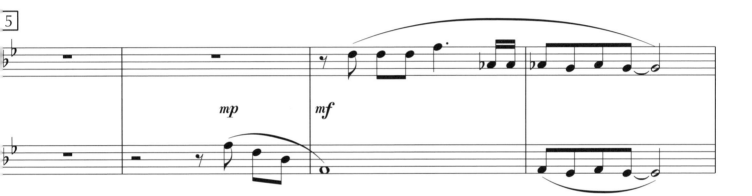

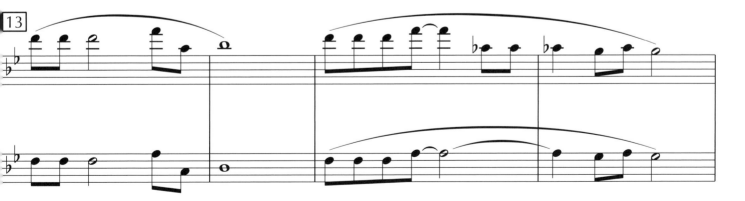

SECONDO

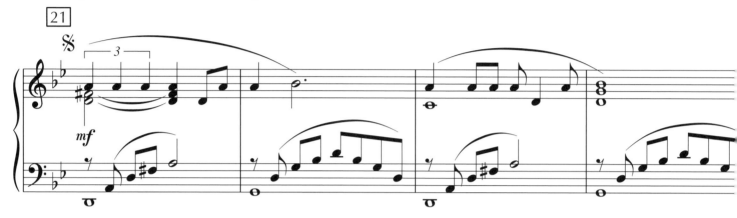

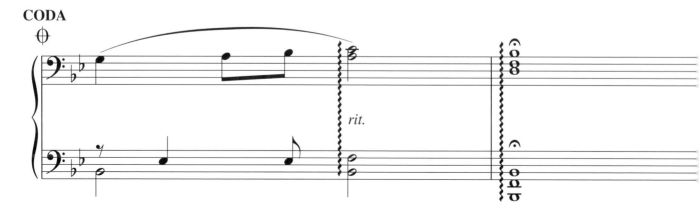

PRIMO

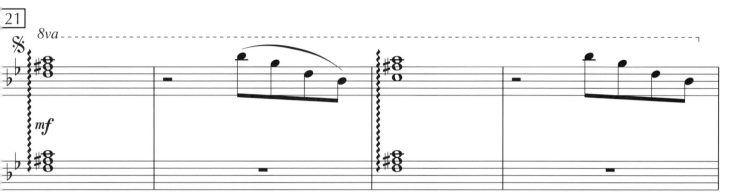

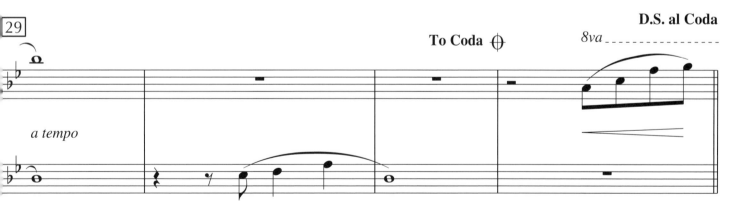

CODA

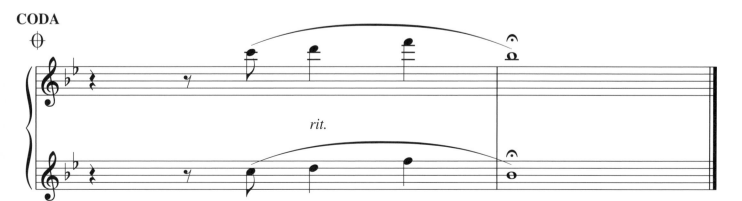

Piano for Two

A VARIETY OF PIANO DUETS FROM HAL LEONARD

ADELE FOR PIANO DUET

Eight of Adele's biggest hits arranged especially for intermediate piano duet! Featuring: Chasing Pavements • Hello • Make You Feel My Love • Rolling in the Deep • Set Fire to the Rain • Skyfall • Someone Like You • When We Were Young.

00172162...................................$14.99

CONTEMPORARY DISNEY DUETS

8 Disney piano duets to play and perform with a friend! Includes: Almost There • He's a Pirate • I See the Light • Let It Go • Married Life • That's How You Know • Touch the Sky • We Belong Together.

00128259 ....$12.99

BILLY JOEL FOR PIANO DUET

Includes 8 of the Piano greatest hits. Perfect as encores, or just for fun! Just the Way You Are • Longest Time • My Piano Man • She's Al• Woman • Uptown Girl • more.

00141139 ....$

THE BEATLES PIANO DUETS – 2ND EDITION

Features 8 arrangements: Can't Buy Me Love • Eleanor Rigby • Hey Jude • Let It Be • Penny Lane • Something • When I'm Sixty-Four • Yesterday.

00290496...................................$15.99

EASY CLASSICAL DUETS

7 great piano duets to perform at a recital, play-for-fun, or sightread! Titles: By the Beautiful Blue Danube (Strauss) • Eine kleine Nachtmusik (Mozart) • Sleeping Beauty Waltz (Tchaikovsky) • and more.

00145767 Book/Online Audio $10.99

RHAPSODY IN BLU FOR PIANO DUET

George Gershwin
Arranged by Brent Ea
This intimate adap delivers access to adv pianists and provide exciting musical collabo and adventure!

00125150 ....$

CHART HITS FOR EASY DUET

10 great early intermediate pop duets! Play with a friend or with the online audio: All of Me • Grenade • Happy • Hello • Just Give Me a Reason • Roar • Shake It Off • Stay • Stay with Me • Thinking Out Loud.

00159796 Book/Online Audio $12.99

THE SOUND OF MUSIC

9 arrangements from the movie/musical, including: Do-Re-Mi • Edelweiss • Maria • My Favorite Things • So Long, Farewell • The Sound of Music • and more.

00290389...................................$14.99

RIVER FLOWS IN Y AND OTHER SONGS ARRANGED FOR PIANO DUET

10 great songs arrang 1 piano, 4 hands, inc the title song and: All (Piano Guys) • Bella's • Beyond • Chariots • • Dawn • Forrest G Main Title (Feather T • Primavera • Somewh Time • Watermark.

00141055 ....$

HAL LEONARD PIANO DUET PLAY-ALONG SERIES

This great series comes with audio that features separate tracks for the Primo and Secondo parts – perfect for practice and performance! Visit www.halleonard.com for a complete list of titles in the series!

COLDPLAY

Clocks • Paradise • The Scientist • A Sky Full of Stars • Speed of Sound • Trouble • Viva La Vida • Yellow.
00141054...................................$14.99

FROZEN

Do You Want to Build a Snowman? • Fixer Upper • For the First Time in Forever • In Summer • Let It Go • Love Is an Open Door • Reindeer(s) Are Better Than People.
00128260...................................$14.99

JAZZ STANDARDS

All the Things You Are • Bewitched • Cheek to Cheek • Don't Get Around Much Anymore • Georgia on My Mind • In the Mood • It's Only a Paper Moon • Satin Doll • The Way You Look Tonight.
00290577...................................$14.99

STAR WARS

8 intergalactic arrange of *Star Wars* theme late intermediate to advanced piano including: Across the S Cantina Band • Duel Fates • The Imperial (Darth Vader's Them Princess Leia's Theme Wars (Main Theme) Throne Room (And End • Yoda's Theme.

00119405...$

HAL•LEONARD

www.halleonard.com